Manners Matter

Activities to Teach Young People Social Skills

W9-CDP-610

by
Debbie Pincus

illustrated by Judith Prowse Buskirk

Cover by Judy Hierstein

Copyright © 1992, Good Apple

ISBN No. 0-86653-688-4

Printing No. 98765432

Good Apple
1204 Buchanan St., Box 299
Carthage, IL 62321-0299

SIMON & SCHUSTER *A Paramount Communications Company*

To the Memories

Dedicated to the memories of my dad, Dr. William Pincus, and my dear friends Mark Lasky and Laura Penn-Bourget.

Acknowledgements

To my loving family–my husband, Richard Ward; my mother, Reva Pincus; my sister, Arlyne Eisberg; my niece and nephew, Lindsay and Scott Eisberg; and to my newborn son, Jacob Daniel Pincus Ward.

GA1422

About the Author

Debbie Pincus is a psychotherapist in private practice in New York City. She has designed and implemented the Interpersonal Communications Program for use in many public and private schools. Ms. Pincus leads workshops and seminars on effective communication, which have received national recognition. She has been selected for inclusion in Who's Who Among Human Service Professionals and Who's Who Among American Women. She lives in Greenwich Village with her husband, Richard, and her son, Jake.

Ms. Pincus is the author of the books *Sharing, Interactions, Feeling Good About Yourself* and coauthor of *Citizenship* published by Good Apple.

GA1422

Table of Contents

GA1422

GA1422

Introduction

Manners Matter is an activity book that offers students creative, imaginative ways to explore what manners are and are not, why they matter and how to use manners to get more from life. Students will reap the rewards good manners bring at home, in school and in several situations. Young people will also be prepared to join the work force where manners really matter.

The book is divided into nine chapters: What Are Manners? Why Do Manners Matter? Getting to Know One Another, Polite Words and Greetings, More Mannerly Ways, What Are Good Table Manners? What Are Good Telephone Manners? How to Dress for Success, and What Are Good Party Manners? Each chapter begins with an exercise entitled "Keeping on Track." This is a vocabulary page for students to enter new words and to find their meanings. Each "Keeping on Track" has an activity to go with it which should be completed by each student.

Note to Teachers

The students will derive more learning and satisfaction from each experience and concept if discussion precedes the activities. Ask students to share personal experiences. Also ask them to share their open-ended questions, opinions, feelings and insights about the issue being discussed. Follow-up activities are also valuable to their learning process. These can include making class booklets and hanging their writings and illustrated stories and reading them aloud, or class debates. All of these can add to lively discussion and enhanced learning. Make sure to always acknowledge students' opinions and ideas without judgement or criticism.

Note to Students

This activity book will be a fun way to learn about manners. Good manners will help you win friends, feel good about yourself and others, and develop strong social awareness skills. Be sure to discuss and debate the ideas and issues presented with your classmates, teachers and parents, and try to find out how manners matter to you.

Note to Parents

Manners Matter is an activity book for use at home as well as in the classroom. Children love hearing their parents' personal experiences, feelings and opinions. Your involvement with your children can help them learn the value of good manners. Rather than having manners dictated to them, this provides an opportunity for children to gain an understanding of the importance of good manners and begin to explore their use in a comfortable atmosphere.

GA1422

Chapter 1

What Are Manners?

Keeping on Track

When you find a word in this chapter which you don't know, circle it in red and write it below. Then look up the word in the dictionary. Write the meaning next to the word.

Words	Meanings
1. _____	_____
2. _____	_____
3. _____	_____
4. _____	_____
5. _____	_____
6. _____	_____
7. _____	_____
8. _____	_____
9. _____	_____
10. _____	_____
11. _____	_____
12. _____	_____
13. _____	_____
14. _____	_____
15. _____	_____
16. _____	_____
17. _____	_____
18. _____	_____
19. _____	_____
20. _____	_____
21. _____	_____
22. _____	_____
23. _____	_____
24. _____	_____
25. _____	_____

GA1422

Manners Are . . .

What are manners anyway and who decides them? Have a contest with your classmates. When the teacher says "GO," each person should make a list as long as he can, in the time allowed, writing what he believes manners are. For example, manners are the way in which people act towards others. When the teacher says "STOP," each student should count his list and see who has the most. Then make a combined classroom list of everyone's ideas and hang it on the wall. Students can keep adding to the list as new ideas are thought of. On your mark, get set, GO.

Discuss with your teacher, classmates and parents what manners are and who decides them.

GA1422

Please Color Me!

Guess which is the most mannerly response in each row and color that box your favorite color. Discuss your answers with your teacher and classmates.

He must be kidding if he thinks he can play the piano.

You can't play with us!

Would you like to join us?

What a clutz!

Let me help you.

Manners seem to be about sensitivity towards others.

GA1422

Lost in Outer Space

Johnny is lost in outer space. Help Johnny find his way out of this crazy space of ill-mannered Martians. Get him back on the route of helpful, caring, mannerly Martians. This will help him feel good about himself and others and get him back home.

5

Mannerly or Unmannerly?

Circle the unmannerly behavior in each group. Then discuss with your parents, teacher and classmates if you've ever behaved in any of those unmannerly ways and why.

She says "hello."

She greets you with a handshake.

She tattles.

She takes your plates off the table.

He helps carry the bags.

He spits.

He offers to be helpful.

He talks behind anyone's back.

She grabs whatever she can.

She waits her turn.

She interrupts.

She is sensitive to other people's feelings.

He hits and punches when angry.

He is careful not to tease.

He washes his hands before eating.

He returns phone calls.

Manners involve taking responsibility for yourself and being responsive to the feelings of others.

GA1422

Greeting Guests at Home

Awkward Al doesn't know what is mannerly when people arrive at his family's home. Watch what he does in each situation and put a big red X over any that you don't think are correct. Discuss with your classmates, teachers and parents what you believe is the mannerly way.

• An uncle of Al's whom he has not seen in a long time arrives at Al's family's home. Al stays on the couch on which he is sitting and continues reading his book. He glances at his uncle and gives a slight nod.

• Friends of Al's parents arrive in the evening to visit. Al does not come out of his room to say "hello" nor does he come out to say "good night."

• A friend of Al's older sister arrives and wants to play with sister Julie. Al greets her with a big kiss because he has been taught to be friendly to guests.

• Neighbors and acquaintances of Al's parents stop by to say "hello" one Sunday afternoon. Al comes out to the living room, greets them with a smile and handshake and excuses himself into his bedroom.

7

GA1422

Cut It Out

Cut out the pictures below that display good manners. Use the pictures to help make the Good Manners Poster on page 9. With your classmates, hang your poster in your classroom and then make a class booklet with all the students' posters.

8

GA1422

Good Manners Poster

Create a striking poster for your bulletin board and for a classroom booklet called "Good Manners." Use the pictures cut out on page 8 to help illustrate your poster.

Manners Matter
Poster

9

What's Wrong with This Picture?

Look at the picture below. Circle unmannerly behaviors and color the picture. Discuss why the behavior is unmannerly with your classmates, teacher and parents.

How do you think this teacher feels?

10

GA1422

How Polite Is Sara?

Read each situation; then color in a number on the continuum from mannerly to rude which you think best describes Sara's behavior. Discuss.

Sara gave her friend a new toy since Sara used her toy and lost it.

Rude   Mannerly

Sara shouted at her friend for not letting her play because she felt very angry and wanted to express her feelings.

Rude   Mannerly

Sara made the bed she slept in when she spent the night at her best friend's home, even though her friend's mother said not to bother.

Rude   Mannerly

GA1422

Take Notice

Notice your own or other classmates' and friends' good manners. Write down the behavior below and be sure to tell them that you noticed! Remember to congratulate yourself, too.

_____

_____

_____

_____

_____

_____

_____

_____

_____

_____

_____

_____

_____

_____

_____

_____

_____

_____

_____

_____

_____

_____

_____

GA1422

What Manners Are

Cut out or draw pictures to describe examples of good manners. Paste your pictures (or cartoons) or drawings in the box below.

GA1422

What Manners Aren't

Cut out or draw pictures to help describe examples of what manners aren't. Paste your pictures (or cartoons) or drawings in the box below.

GA1422

Chapter 2

Why Do Manners Matter?

GA1422

Keeping on Track

When you find a word in this chapter which you don't know, circle it in red and write it below. Then look up the word in the dictionary. Write the meaning next to the word.

Words	Meaning
1. _____	_____
2. _____	_____
3. _____	_____
4. _____	_____
5. _____	_____
6. _____	_____
7. _____	_____
8. _____	_____
9. _____	_____
10. _____	_____
11. _____	_____
12. _____	_____
13. _____	_____
14. _____	_____
15. _____	_____
16. _____	_____
17. _____	_____
18. _____	_____
19. _____	_____
20. _____	_____
21. _____	_____
22. _____	_____
23. _____	_____
24. _____	_____
25. _____	_____

When you have found all the meanings for the words above, scramble the words and ask your classmates to try to unscramble them and tell you their meanings.

GA1422

Honestly, Max!

Read the cartoon strip. Max is being very honest about the way he feels. So what is the problem?

Discuss with your teacher, classmates and parents when being honest with your feelings is not mannerly. What do manners have to do with feelings and sensitivity toward others? Remember it is OK to have negative feelings about others, but in certain times and situations it is best to keep them to yourself!

Circle the situations below in which honest feelings would be best kept to yourself.

in front of lots of people

when you don't know the person

when you could insult and embarrass a person

Manners matter because they have to do with feelings and sensitivity.

GA1422

Manners vs. Demands

Help Jake understand how manners are more helpful than tantrums in getting what he wants. List the reasons below.

1. Manners don't turn other people off.
2. People can hear what you want when you're not screaming.
3.
4.
5.

Manners matter because they help people get what they want.

GA1422

What Might a Person Feel If...

What do you think the older woman in Picture A feels? Write all the feeling words that you can think of that might describe her feelings. Use the list on page 20, to help you identify words which describe feelings.

What do you think the older woman in Picture B feels? Write all the feeling words you can think of that might describe her feelings. Again, use the list to help you find words for feelings.

Discuss with your teacher, classmates and parents what manners have to do with feelings.

Feeling Words

_____

_____

_____

_____

_____

Feeling Words

_____

_____

_____

_____

_____

Feeling Words

sad	happy	frustrated
jealous	loving	relieved
curious	anxious	sympathetic
shocked	hurt	disappointed
apologetic	bored	guilty
miserable	enraged	frightened
	embarrassed	

GA1422

Stay Away or Come Close

Good manners help others to want to be around you. Color each picture that displays behaviors that would make you want to be with a person.

Manners matter because they help people want to be with you.

21

GA1422

Mind Your Manners, Tyler

Help Tyler mind his manners. Whisper in his ear what would be good manners in the situation below.

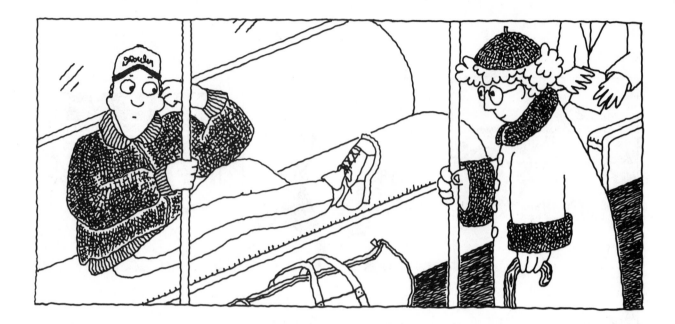

Discuss with your teacher, classmates and parents how manners are really about good citizenship, respect for others and consideration and responsibility.

Why do you think an older person should get a seat on a bus? A pregnant person? A sick person? A person with lots of bags in his/her arms? A person carrying a stroller and an infant? Manners are for reasons.

> Manners matter because they have to do with being a good citizen
> and with respect and consideration.

So What If Manners Matter

Sammy doesn't always feel like being mannerly. He doesn't always feel like being nice to others. Help Sammy understand how using good manners will help him to feel good about himself and others.

Finish each statement below.

Good manners help you to be polite.

If you are polite, then others will _____.

If others are polite to me, then I might feel _____.

Good manners help you be a considerate person.

If you are a considerate person, then others will _____.

If others are considerate of me, then I might feel _____.

Good manners help you be caring.

If you are caring towards others, then others will _____.

If others are caring to me, then I might feel _____.

Good manners make others want to be with you.

If others want to be with me, then I might feel _____.

Good manners help you treat others respectfully.

If you treat others respectfully, then others will _____.

If others treat me respectfully, then I might feel _____.

Discuss with your teacher, classmates and parents some of the benefits of using good manners. How might good manners help you feel good about yourself and others?

Manners matter because they can help you feel good about yourself and others.

GA1422

Why Do Manners Matter?

Put an X in the boxes that explain good reasons for good manners. Try to get tic-tac-toe (X's in a straight line or diagonally). Discuss your reasons with your teacher, classmates and parents. Remember "good reasons" mean reasons that help you to feel good about yourself and others.

Manners matter because teachers won't bug you.	Manners matter because they show respect for others.	Manners matter because no one will bother you.
Manners matter because you can get your parents to give you more allowance.	Manners matter because they help you feel good about yourself.	Manners matter because they improve your grades.
Manners matter because they help get your homework done.	Manners matter because they help you care and feel for others.	Manners matter because they keep you from getting sick.

GA1422

Stares

There are people who get stared at frequently. How do you think they feel? How would you feel?

How might the person who is being stared at feel?

_____

_____

Discuss with your teacher, classmates and parents what is rude about staring. Why do people do it? Have you ever been stared at? How did you feel?

Manners matter because without them people might feel like outcasts.

GA1422

Consideration and Manners

How is Willy being inconsiderate in each scene? Can you help him be considerate by teaching him the proper manners in each situation?

Teach Willy manners that will help him be more considerate. Write them below.

GA1422

Gossip

Read the gossip going on.

1. Did you hear that Katy didn't do her homework last night and got in trouble?

2. Guess what I heard? Katy didn't do her homework and might get suspended.

3. Wait until I tell you what I heard. Katy was found kissing some guy and is in big trouble.

4. You won't believe what I heard. Katy got thrown out of school for something terrible she must have done.

5. Katy is a troublemaker. I don't think we better hang around with her.

6. Yeah! I've heard some weird stories about Katy!

What is gossip?_____

Why is gossip considered unmannerly? _____

What problems can gossip create, as it did for Katy?_____

How is gossip unfair to the person it is about?_____

Why do you think people have the need to gossip? _____

Have you ever gossiped? What was your need? _____

Have you ever been gossiped about? How did it make you feel? What trouble did it

create for you? _____

Manners matter because they protect others from being unfairly talked about.

GA1422

Hurts

Bad manners can cause people's feelings to be hurt. Teasing, staring, ignoring, making fun of, name-calling, and gossiping are just some bad manners that affect others' feelings.

Pretend a new student arrives in your class. In the pictures below notice the new students. Write a bad-mannered "hello" toward him or her and in the third panel a good-mannered "hello." Discuss these welcomes with your teacher and classmates.

New Student	Bad-Mannered "Hello"	Good-Mannered "Hello"

Manners matter because they help people from having their feelings hurt.

GA1422

Have You Ever Been...

Fill in the blanks.

Have you ever teased someone? Why? _____

Have you ever been teased? How did you feel? _____

Have you ever ignored someone? Why? _____

Have you ever been ignored? How did you feel? _____

Have you ever stared at someone? Why? _____

Have you ever been made fun of? How did you feel? _____

Have you ever called someone a bad name? Why?_____

Have you ever been called a bad name? How did you feel? _____

Good manners include kindness, sensitivity, care and respect. Look up the definitions of each of these words and discuss their meanings with your teacher, classmates and parents.

Kindness_____

Sensitivity _____

Care_____

Respect _____

Manners matter because they have to do with kindness,
sensitivity, care and respect.

GA1422

Write and Tell

Fill in the blanks.

Write about a time you were kind to someone. _____

_____

_____

How did you feel? _____

_____

_____

Write about a time when someone was kind to you? How did you feel? _____

_____

_____

Write about a time when you were sensitive to someone. How did you feel? _____

_____

_____

Write about a time someone was sensitive to you. How did you feel? _____

_____

_____

Write about a time you cared about someone. How did you feel? _____

_____

_____

Write about a time someone cared about you. How did you feel? _____

_____

_____

Tell about these special times to your classmates, teachers and parents.

GA1422

What's the Connection?

What do manners have to do with consideration?

_____

_____

_____

_____

What do manners have to do with feelings?

_____

_____

_____

_____

What do manners have to do with respect?

_____

_____

_____

_____

GA1422

How Polite Is Jesse?

Read each situation, then color in a number on the continuum from mannerly to rude which you think best describes Jesse's behavior. Discuss.

Jesse finally reached across the dinner table to get a bread roll since Luke kept ignoring his request to pass them.

2   4   6   8   10

Rude   Mannerly

Jesse did not buy his friend Mike a present for his birthday since Jesse could not attend Mike's birthday (although he was invited).

2   4   6   8   10

Rude   Mannerly

Jesse shook his opponent's hand and congratulated him for playing a good game even though Jesse's team came in last.

2   4   6   8   10

Rude   Mannerly

GA1422

Write and Illustrate

Write a story. Include each of the words below. Illustrate your story on the back. Make a class booklet of everyone's stories.

sensitive	tease	respect	helpful
ignore	kindness	encourage	gossip
care	stare	jealous	

_____

_____

_____

_____

_____

_____

_____

_____

_____

_____

_____

_____

_____

_____

_____

_____

_____

_____

_____

_____

GA1422

Chapter 3

Getting to Know One Another

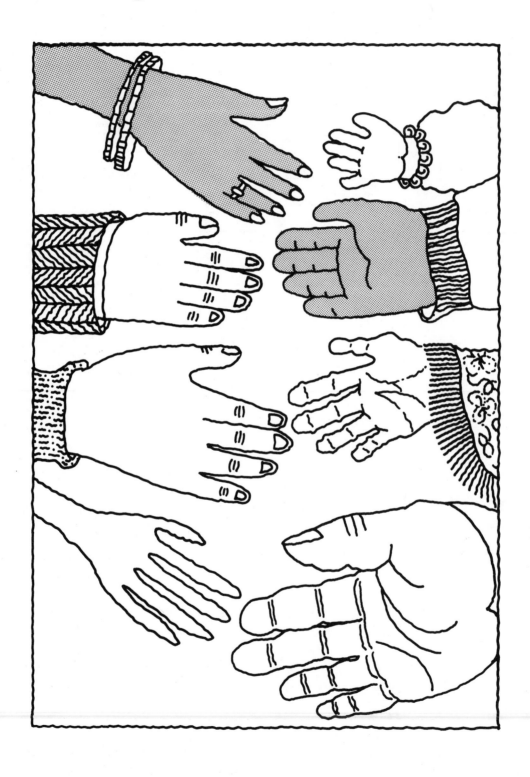

GA1422

Keeping on Track

When you find a word in this chapter which you don't know, circle it in red and write it below. Then look up the word in the dictionary. Write the meaning next to the word.

Words	Meaning
1.	
2.	
3.	
4.	
5.	
6.	
7.	
8.	
9.	
10.	
11.	
12.	
13.	
14.	
15.	
16.	
17.	
18.	
19.	
20.	
21.	
22.	
23.	
24.	
25.	

When you have found all the meanings to the words above, scramble your words and ask classmates to try to unscramble. Use a separate sheet of paper.

GA1422

Introductions

Let's begin by having you introduce yourself. Always remember to say "hello," your name and to ask the other person's (or persons') name.

Fill in the blanks below.

_____. My name is _____. What is/are

your _____?

Fill in the word balloons over the characters' heads. Remember, one character is you and the other is the person you are meeting.

Circle which behavior in each line is most appropriate when you are introducing yourself.

1. stand up	sit down	lie down
2. look person in the feet	look person in the eyes	look person in the stomach
3. mumble	speak loudly and clearly	whisper
4. shake hands	tickle other person's hand	arm wrestle other person

GA1422

Meeting Others

Now that you've learned to introduce yourself you want to know how to introduce others.

Questions

Do you think you should introduce both first and last names? _____

Do you think you should introduce a man before a woman? _____

Do you think you should introduce a child before an adult? _____

Do you think you should introduce an older person before a younger person? _____

Do you think you should introduce a person you like before someone you don't like?

_____

Do you think if you do not hear or understand a person's name you can ask again?

_____

Proper etiquette says to introduce an older person before a younger person; a girl before a boy; an adult before a child and a woman before a man; to use both first and last names; and to ask again if you don't understand, hear or remember a name.

So give it a try. You are with your classmate Martha, an elderly woman named Matilda, and your father Arthur.

_____. My name is _____. I'd like to introduce you to

_____ and _____ and

_____.

Look up the word *etiquette* in the dictionary. What does it mean? _____

_____

How do you feel about following the rules of etiquette when introducing yourself and others? _____

What might be helpful about knowing these rules? _____

_____

GA1422

Making Conversation

When you are introduced to someone, don't just stand there and twiddle your thumbs. Say something. Try to make conversation. The person introducing you should tell something about you so you have a start as to what to talk about. When someone tells you about a person, ask questions.

Try it. Fill in the balloons.

38

GA1422

What Happens If...

What happens if...

You are with one friend and someone else walks over to play with you. You have forgotten this other person's name. Should you...

____ tell the people you have forgotten his/her name?
____ make up a name and hope it is the right one?
____ skip introductions and just keep playing or talking?

Proper etiquette says to say that you say you are sorry, but you have forgotten his/her name. Then the person whose name has been forgotten should introduce himself/herself to the friend. So don't panic. You are allowed to forget. We are human.

What happens if...

You are with one friend and you meet up with a large group of kids that you know, but your friend does not know. Should you...

____ say every person's name in the large group?
____ just say a few persons' names?
____ just introduce your friend by saying his/her name and then let the others introduce themselves?

If it is a small group then you can say everyone's name.

What happens if...

You are introducing your friend to a grown-up. Should you...

____ introduce the grown-up by her first name since that is what you call her?
____ introduce her by her last name only?

Proper etiquette says to introduce grown-ups by their last names unless the grown-ups say it is all right to call them by their first names.

GA1422

Handshakes

When you meet someone and introduce yourself, a handshake is a polite greeting. Practice with your classmates giving a good handshake. Then have a contest for the best handshaker.

Dos of Handshakes	**Don'ts of Handshakes**
short	be wishy washy
firm	hold on too long
dry	crush the other person's hand
solid	be slippery and wet

Handshakes communicate although no words are used. What does a good handshake say to you? _____

_____

What do you communicate to someone when you give a good handshake? _____

_____

Fill in and cut out your ballot for the best handshaker. Give to your teacher.

****

My vote for the best handshaker in the class is _____

I have selected him/her because his/her handshake is _____

_____

_____

****

GA1422

Chapter 4

Polite Words and Greetings

GA1422

Keeping on Track

When you find a word in this chapter which you don't know, circle it in red and write it below. Then look up the word in the dictionary. Write the meaning next to the word.

Words	Meaning
1. _____	_____
2. _____	_____
3. _____	_____
4. _____	_____
5. _____	_____
6. _____	_____
7. _____	_____
8. _____	_____
9. _____	_____
10. _____	_____
11. _____	_____
12. _____	_____
13. _____	_____
14. _____	_____
15. _____	_____
16. _____	_____
17. _____	_____
18. _____	_____
19. _____	_____
20. _____	_____
21. _____	_____
22. _____	_____
23. _____	_____
24. _____	_____
25. _____	_____

Use each word in a sentence once you know its meaning. See if your classmates can figure out the meaning of the word just by hearing it in your sentence. Use a separate sheet of paper to write your sentences.

GA1422

Polite Words

Make a list of all the polite words or greetings you can think of. See how many you can use each day.

Example:
How do you do?
Please.

_____	_____	_____
_____	_____	_____
_____	_____	_____
_____	_____	_____
_____	_____	_____
_____	_____	_____
_____	_____	_____
_____	_____	_____
_____	_____	_____
_____	_____	_____
_____	_____	_____
_____	_____	_____
_____	_____	_____
_____	_____	_____
_____	_____	_____
_____	_____	_____
_____	_____	_____
_____	_____	_____
_____	_____	_____

When you have completed your list (at least for now), create a word search using the words and phrases you have listed. Make your word search on page 44. Give it to a classmate to try.

GA1422

Create a Word Search

Using the list of polite words and phrases on page 43, fill in the grid below creating your own word search for a classmate. Put one letter of each word in a box going across, down or diagonally. Your next word or phrase can join any letter from the other words on the grid. Fill in the leftover blocks with any letters.

For example:

P	L	E	A	S	E		
					X		
					C		
					U		
T	H	A	N	K	S		
					E		
					M		
					E		

See how many polite words and phrases your classmates can find in your word search. Have them circle each word they find.

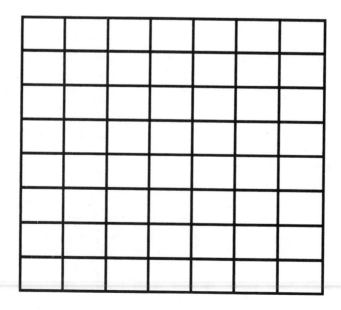

Thank You

Look at all the thank-you's Sue said to her parents today. Read them and decide why they are necessary between people.

Thanks, Dad, for making sure that I got to school on time today.

Mom, thank you for making my lunch.

Thank you for helping me understand my geography. I was able to participate in the discussion at school.

Look up the word *appreciation* in your dictionary. Write its definition.

_____

Why do you believe that it is necessary to share your appreciation of someone?

_____

How does it make you feel? _____

How does it make the other person feel? _____

What does it do for your relationship? _____

_____

GA1422

Other Thank-you's

Thank someone after you
  visit his home
  sleep over
  eat dinner over
  go to his party
  receive a gift from him
Or write a thank-you note. Say something about your appreciation of his gift or how you used or will use it. Always say something nice.

You can thank him in words or write a thank-you note to someone that you would like to thank for something. Send or give him your note.

Send people cards to help them know you are thinking of them. Especially do this on birthdays, on holidays or other special occasions.

Dear _____,

                                                                    Love,

GA1422

What's Wrong?

Rebecca is using polite words. Why are people getting annoyed with her? Discuss with your teacher and classmates.

Rebecca said *excuse me*, *please* and *thank you*—so what's the problem? We can use polite words and phrases in impolite ways but then they are no longer polite.

47

GA1422

How Polite Is Amanda?

Read each situation. Then color in a number on the continuum from mannerly to rude which you think best describes Amanda. Discuss.

Amanda apologized to her brother for interrupting him while he was speaking.

2   4   6   8   10
Rude   Mannerly

Amanda did not say "thank you" to the cab driver because she did not think he drove safely.

2   4   6   8   10
Rude   Mannerly

Amanda answered the telephone. The person calling asked to speak to Amanda's mother. Even though Amanda's mother was right next to her, she told the person on the phone her mother wasn't home because that is what her mom told her to say.

2   4   6   8   10
Rude   Mannerly

GA1422

Bubble Fun

Color the illustration above and discuss with your teacher, classmates and parents which, if any, child is showing good manners and why. If either child is not, what would be mannerly behavior in this situation?

49

After You

Sometimes people say "After you." The phrase usually is considered to be polite. Think of all the situations in which it would be polite to think of others before you think of yourself. Write them below and make a book called *After You*. Illustrate.

For example: Offering others food before yourself

_____
_____
_____
_____
_____
_____
_____
_____
_____
_____
_____
_____
_____
_____
_____
_____
_____
_____
_____
_____
_____
_____
_____
_____

GA1422

I'm Sorry

Circle all the situations in which you would need to say "I'm sorry." Add more of your own.

If someone you know has had a death of someone close to him (animals included)

If you are having fun

If your friend's parents get divorced

If you hurt someone else's feelings

When you can't include someone in a game because you already have enough players

When you have won the main part in a school play and friends are congratulating you

_____

_____

_____

_____

_____

_____

_____

GA1422

Excuse Me

Think of all the situations when it may be polite to say "excuse me." Write them below and make a booklet entitled *Excuse Me*. Illustrate.

For example: When I sneeze or cough

_____

_____

_____

_____

_____

_____

_____

_____

_____

_____

_____

_____

_____

_____

_____

_____

_____

_____

_____

_____

_____

_____

_____

GA1422

Chapter 5

More Mannerly Ways

GA1422

Keeping on Track

When you find a word in this chapter which you don't know, circle it in red and write it below. Then look up the word in the dictionary. Write the meaning next to the word.

Words	Meaning
1.	
2.	
3.	
4.	
5.	
6.	
7.	
8.	
9.	
10.	
11.	
12.	
13.	
14.	
15.	
16.	
17.	
18.	
19.	
20.	
21.	
22.	
23.	
24.	
25.	

Write a story using as many of your words as you can *after* you know their meanings. Read your story aloud. Use a separate sheet of paper.

GA1422

Smiles

Draw a smile in each blank face below. What difference do you think a smile makes? Discuss.

Please Let Me Finish What I'm Saying!

What's wrong with this picture?

Discuss with your teacher, classmates and parents the problems in the interactions above. Who is not using good manners? What is not mannerly about this person's actions? How might you feel if you were the little boy? Why do you think good manners include speaking when the other person has finished speaking? Why is interrupting considered poor manners?

Make a list of all the ways you can think of that the boy can respond to the girl. Discuss with your teacher and classmates which responses would be most effective and which would show good manners. Are they the same?

GA1422

Me! Me! Me!

Andie likes a lot of attention, and he likes it when he wants it! Watch him in action below. Have you ever felt like Andie?

We all feel like Andie at times. And there is nothing wrong with his need to want and love attention. We all do. However what Andie has to learn is that he is not the only one around or the only one who has needs. Andie may want to have Dad play with him, but perhaps Dad is tired and just came home from work. Andie has to learn to politely ask for what he wants without demanding and interrupting others. Can you help him? Put words in the word balloons that will help him ask for what he wants without interrupting. Share your completed cartoons with your classmates, teacher and parents.

57

GA1422

Getting into Your Shoes

Draw yourself in Zachary's shoes. How would you feel if you were being spoken to the way he is? Change any statement that sounds rude to you so it is said in a more polite and sensitive way. Use the following polite words to choose from.

Please   Thank you   You're welcome

Pass me the butter.

Hurry up.

Give me that toy!

Always imagine yourself in someone else's shoes in order to help you feel what he/she might feel. If it doesn't feel so good, think of more mannerly ways you can better behave so that the other person feels treated respectfully.

Treat others the way you'd want to be treated.

Thanks for sharing your lunch with me.

Knock Them Down

Try to knock all the pins down by the end of the day. When you accomplish what a pin suggests, put an *X* over it. By the time you have an *X* over each of the bowling pins, you have shown excellent manners. Play again the next day.

I said "thank you" at least three times today.

I asked someone who was alone to join us.

I did not interrupt anyone today.

I shared my books and toys.

I offered to help someone today.

I used good table manners.

I greeted others properly at least one time today.

I said "please" at least two times today.

I did not push when standing in line.

I waited my turn even though I felt impatient.

I listened to someone else as well as asking in a polite way to be listened to.

I apologized when I needed to be responsible for my actions.

I did not gossip about anyone today.

I offered my seat to someone else.

I asked someone else how his day was.

59

GA1422

Excuses, Excuses

Derrick gets shoved by Kyle while waiting in line. Derrick screams out, "How come you didn't say 'sorry'?"

Help Kyle think of as many excuses as possible for not using his manners.

Examples of excuses:

I have to get back to class.

I didn't see you.

You were in MY way.

You shoved me yesterday.

_____

_____

_____

_____

_____

_____

_____

_____

_____

_____

_____

_____

_____

_____

_____

_____

_____

_____

GA1422

Apologies

How would you feel if you were the person being tripped? _____

How would you feel if you were the person being tripped? _____

_____

Do you imagine that an apology can make you feel better? Explain.

_____

_____

_____

_____

_____

_____

GA1422

Apology Mosaic

Color this mosaic using the color chart below.

Color the spaces showing manners RED.
Color the spaces showing lack of manners YELLOW.
Color the lines in between BLACK.

Jesse's favorite toy was broken when his group of friends borrowed it. Color the mannerly responses to Jesse RED and the unmannerly responses YELLOW.

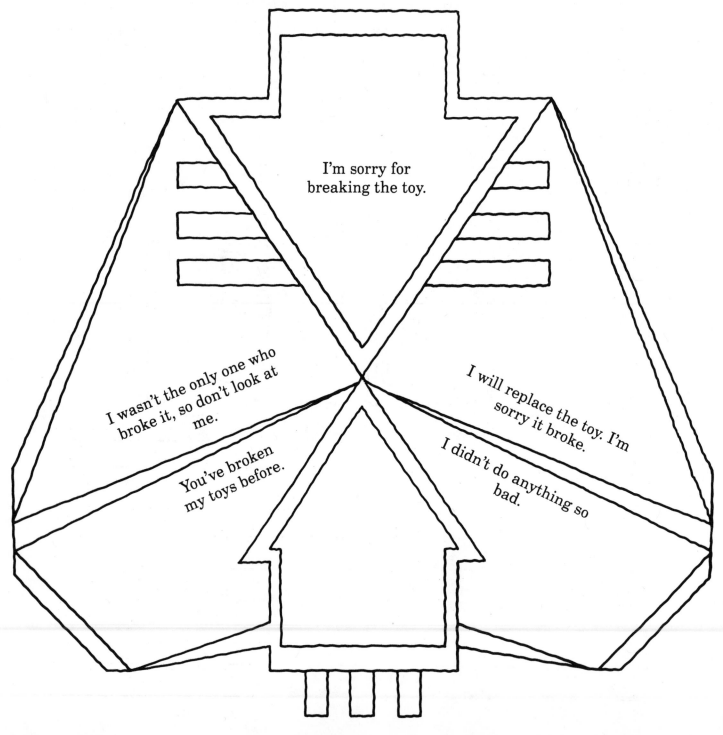

62

GA1422

Rewriting the Story

Think of a time that you felt you were owed an apology from someone and you did not receive it. Think of the person who owed it to you and the situation. Write the story below, but this time write the ending the way you would have liked it (getting the apology you would have liked). If you were never in this situation, make up a story. Read the stories aloud.

_____

_____

_____

_____

_____

_____

_____

_____

_____

_____

_____

_____

_____

_____

_____

_____

_____

_____

_____

_____

_____

_____

_____

How do you feel now that you received the apology?

GA1422

How Polite Is Alex?

Read each situation, then color in a number on the continuum from mannerly to rude which you think best describes Alex's behavior. Discuss.

Alex tells his friend that he doesn't want to play with him today. He'd rather read his book for the upcoming history test.

Alex tells his friend on the playground to get lost because he smells.

Alex tells his friend that he will play with him if his friend will buy him an ice-cream cone.

GA1422

The Third Wheel

What do you think it means to be a "third wheel"? Did you ever feel like a "third wheel"? What made you feel left out? Watch the interactions below and see if you understand why Max feels left out or like the third wheel. Discuss with your teacher, classmates and parents how Sam and Gary are not using good manners when they treat others like a third wheel.

65

GA1422

Building Blocks

Cut out the blocks on this page that would lay the foundation to building good manners. Paste them in any design you'd like on page 67. Look up any word for which you do not know the meaning.

Self-righteousness	**Hate**	**Respect**
Equality	**Sensitivity**	**Prejudice**
Social Conscience	**Obedience**	**Freedom**
Vanity	**Discrimination**	**Love**
Snobbery	**Loyalty**	**Care**
Self-knowledge	**Tolerance**	**Rebelliousness**

GA1422

Building Blocks to Good Manners

Paste your blocks from page 66 here in any design you wish. Color and hang your designs.

GA1422

How Polite Is Jennifer?

Read each situation. Then color in a number on the continuum from mannerly to rude which you think best describes Jennifer's behavior. Discuss.

Jennifer spills milk on the floor and won't clean it up. Then Jennifer yells to her mother, "Kate made me spill it since she was teasing me."

Rude   2   4   6   8   10   Mannerly

Jennifer offers to help clean up after the party because she knows how much work her mother put into making this party.

Rude   2   4   6   8   10   Mannerly

Jennifer offers to share her new toy with her friend as long as her friend in return promises to share something of hers in return.

Rude   2   4   6   8   10   Mannerly

GA1422

Write On!

Choose a title below and write a story. Read it to your teacher and classmates.

The Tattletale   The Cheater

The Bad Sport   The Leader

The Gossiper   The Most Popular Kid in the Class

The Humiliator

_____

_____

_____

_____

_____

_____

_____

_____

_____

_____

_____

_____

_____

_____

_____

_____

_____

_____

_____

_____

_____

GA1422

Chapter 6

What Are Good Table Manners?

Keeping on Track

When you find a word in this chapter which you don't know, circle it in red and write it below. Then look up the word in the dictionary. Write the meaning next to the word.

Words	Meaning
1. _____	_____
2. _____	_____
3. _____	_____
4. _____	_____
5. _____	_____
6. _____	_____
7. _____	_____
8. _____	_____
9. _____	_____
10. _____	_____
11. _____	_____
12. _____	_____
13. _____	_____
14. _____	_____
15. _____	_____
16. _____	_____
17. _____	_____
18. _____	_____
19. _____	_____
20. _____	_____
21. _____	_____
22. _____	_____
23. _____	_____
24. _____	_____
25. _____	_____

Make a word search using your words *once* you know their meanings. See if your classmates can successfully find each word in the word search.

GA1422

Setting the Table

Help Mom and Dad set the table for your family's Saturday afternoon lunch. Cut out the utensils on page 73 and paste them correctly on the table below. Make the proper table setting in front of Mom. You'll find the proper place setting shown on page 74.

GA1422

Utensils

Cut out the utensils and paste them correctly on the dinner table on page 72.

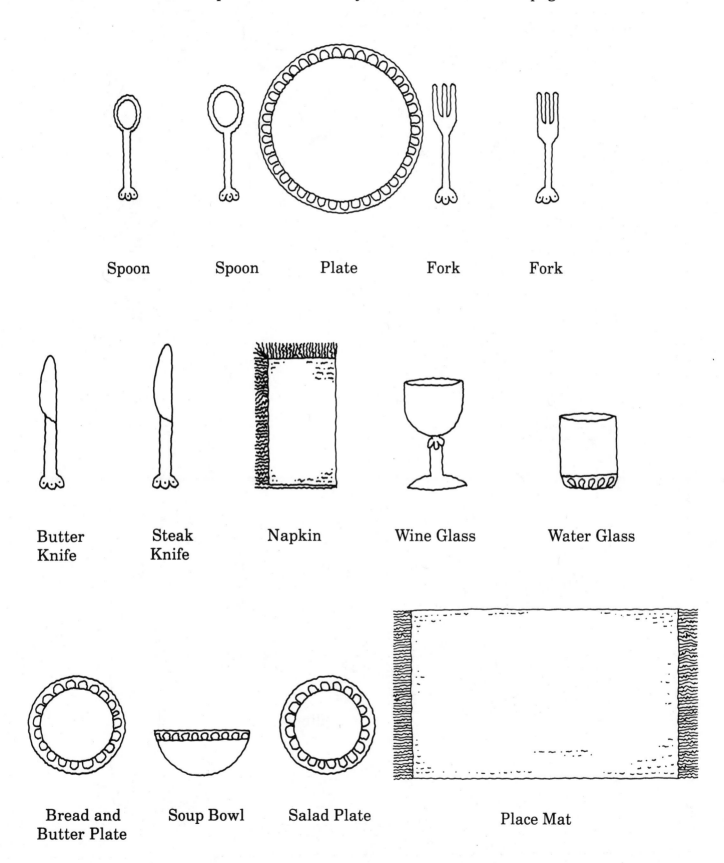

Spoon   Spoon   Plate   Fork   Fork

Butter Knife   Steak Knife   Napkin   Wine Glass   Water Glass

Bread and Butter Plate   Soup Bowl   Salad Plate   Place Mat

Informal and Formal Table Place Settings

Here's a place setting for *informal* dining.

(Eating at home on a Saturday afternoon)

Here's a place setting for more *formal* dining.

(Christmas dinner)

Begin eating with the flatware furthest from your plate.

74

GA1422

Napkin Manners

Look over the list. Then under the *Dos* column, list all proper ways to use your napkin. Under *Don'ts* write all the improper ways.

Leave your napkin under your fork throughout your meal.

Open your napkin and put it on your lap.

Wipe your mouth with your napkin and then put it back on the table.

Sneeze into your napkin and put it back on the table.

When leaving the table during a meal, place your napkin on the chair, not back on the table.

When you are finished eating, pick up your napkin and place it on the table to the left of your plate.

Dos	Don'ts

Why do you think napkin manners are important?

GA1422

Cut It Out, Please

Cut out the pictures that show good table manners and paste them around the table on page 77. Discuss with your teacher, classmates and parents what is unmannerly about the pictures you did not paste around the table.

A Mannerly Table

Paste the mannerly pictures from page 76 around this table. Then discuss with your teacher, classmates and parents the behaviors that display good table manners.

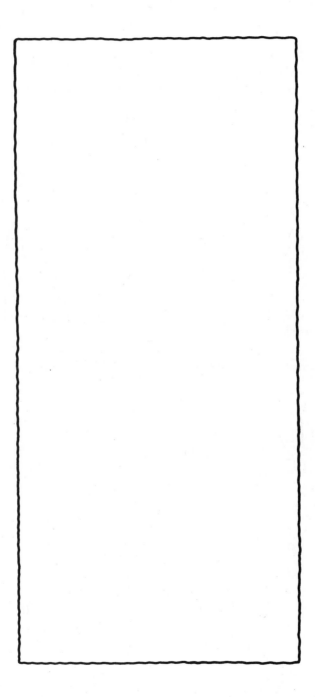

GA1422

What Is Wrong with This Picture?

Look at the picture below. Circle unmannerly behaviors and discuss with your teacher, classmates and parents why they are unmannerly.

78

Design a Mosaic

Color the boxes according to the key below.

Key
Blue—boxes describing good table manners
Orange—boxes describing poor table manners

Sneezing into food	Grabbing food off someone else's plate	Helping clear the table	Excusing yourself to go to the bathroom
Chomping loudly on food	Asking for food to be passed	Chewing with mouth open	Sitting with a straight back so that you can breathe easily
Telling a disgusting story while others are eating	Feet on the floor	Asking if anyone wants the last piece of food that you've already had	Tickling someone while he is eating
Passing all serving dishes to the right	When serving yourself from a platter with a serving fork and spoon, put the spoon under your portion and use the fork to hold it in place as you put it on your plate.	Waiting until everyone is seated before you begin eating	When serving yourself, take only the amount of food you know you can eat.

GA1422

Where Should My Silverware Go?

Proper etiquette tells us that when we are resting between bites we should place our flatware like this:

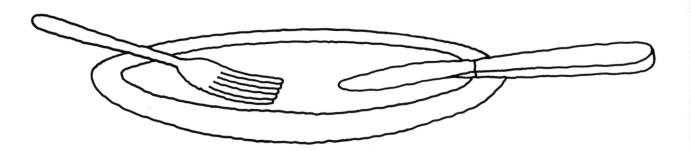

When we have finished eating, we should place our flatware like this:

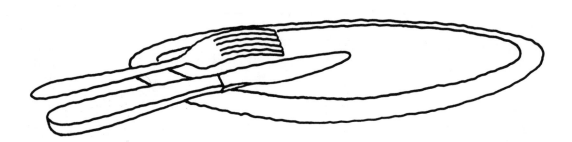

Why might these rules of flatware etiquette be helpful to us in a restaurant?

_____

When we are eating?_____

Don't
stab your food
bang your silverware against your plate

GA1422

Be a Table Manners Detective

Taylor has excellent table manners. Be a detective and see what observations you can make about Taylor and his behaviors. Write your observations below.

What do you notice about Taylor's posture at the table? _____

What do you notice about Taylor's silverware at the table? _____

What do you notice about Taylor's mouth at the table? _____

What do you notice about the way Taylor sits at the table? _____

What other behaviors do you notice about Taylor at the table? _____

_____

_____

Discuss good table manners with your teacher, classmates and parents.

GA1422

On Your Mark...Get Set...Go

Have a contest with your classmates. You have four minutes to write a list of all the reasons you can think of that table manners matter. Then compare your lists with your classmates and see who has come up with the longest list. Compile your lists into one long list to be hung on the bulletin board. On your mark...get set...go.

<u>Good table manners help us digest our food properly.</u>

_____

_____

_____

_____

_____

_____

_____

_____

_____

_____

GA1422

Drippy Foods

Color the illustration above and discuss with your teacher, classmates and parents which child, if any, is showing good manners and why. If not, what would be mannerly behavior in this situation?

83

GA1422

Be a Keen Observer

Observe each person at the dinner table. Color each box red if he/she is using good table manners. Next to each name write what is proper about his/her table behavior.

Jennifer
She turns away from the table to sneeze and cough and covers her mouth.

Alex
He burps and laughs rather than excusing himself.

Suzanne
She blows her nose with her napkin.

Carol
She keeps up good conversation throughout the meal.

Dad
He picks his teeth after eating and reads the newspaper while eating.

Mom
She places her napkin on the table as she leaves.

Billy
He burps and says "excuse me."

Jeryl
She thanks the hostess and compliments her on the delicious meal.

Cary
She makes lots of noises with lips while eating.

Lauren
She leaves the table before everyone is finished and does not ask permission.

Billy_____

Jeryl _____

Cary _____

Lauren _____

Jennifer _____

Alex_____

Suzanne_____

Mom _____

Dad _____

Carol_____

Noisy Drinks

Color the illustration above and discuss with your teacher, classmates and parents which child, if any, is showing manners and why. If not, what would be mannerly behavior in this situation?

85

GA1422

Chapter 7

What Are Good Telephone Manners?

Keeping on Track

When you find a word in this chapter which you don't know, circle it in red and write it below. Then look up the word in the dictionary. Write the meaning next to the word.

Words	Meaning
1.	
2.	
3.	
4.	
5.	
6.	
7.	
8.	
9.	
10.	
11.	
12.	
13.	
14.	
15.	
16.	
17.	
18.	
19.	
20.	
21.	
22.	
23.	
24.	
25.	

Make up a word game to play with your classmates once you know the meanings of the words. Use all the words above. Use a separate sheet of paper.

GA1422

Bingo

What are good manners when making a telephone call? Put an *X* over each box which describes good telephone manners. See if you can get a BINGO by having *X's* in boxes down or across.

B	I	N	G	O
Just say "Hello"; wait until the person asks "Who would you like to speak with?"	If you get a wrong number, apologize and then say "Good-bye" and hang up.	**FREE**	Mumble and whisper.	Ask for person you are calling to speak to.
Have a long conversation with whoever picks up the phone.	Say, "Hello."	Don't say "Hello." Just ask for the person you are calling.	If person is not at home, slam the phone down in frustration.	Always say "Good-bye" before hanging up.
If you get a wrong number, just quickly hang up on the person.	If the person you are calling for is not there, leave a message or say "'Thank you, good-bye!"	Don't give your name or number if the person is not home.	You don't have to say good-bye if the person you wanted to speak to is not home.	Give your name.

88

Telephone Etiquette

What's unmannerly with these telephone conversations? Explain below.

1. Doug: Hello, is your brother at home?
   Greg: No. (Slams the phone down)
   What is unmannerly in Greg's conversation and/or behavior?

   _____

   _____

   Rewrite a more polite conversation between Doug and Greg.
   Doug: Hello, is your brother at home?

   Greg: No, _____

   _____

   _____

   _____

   _____

   _____

2. Sally: Hello, is this Jean?
   Jean: Yes it is.
   Sally: How are you? This is Sally.
   Jean: Yeah. What do you want? Why did you call?
   What is unmannerly in Jean's conversation?

   _____

   _____

   Rewrite a more polite conversation between Sally and Jean.
   Sally: Hello, is this Jean?
   Jean: Yes it is.
   Sally: How are you? This is Sally.

   Jean: _____

   _____

   _____

   _____

   _____

   _____

GA1422

Leaving Messages

Leave a mannerly message on your friend's answering machine.

_____. This is _____. I'm calling to speak with

_____.

_____, please call me at _____ when you get

home _____.

****

You answer the phone and the call is for your mother. Make sure to leave her a clear message with all the information she will need. What do you need to tell her?

Who called? _____

For _____

Time _____

Person's phone # _____

Message _____

****

You are on the telephone and you hear your call waiting signal (if you have it). What should you do? A or B

A. You: Excuse me, Sara. I'll get right back to you.

   You: (go to call waiting call) Hello, Tess. I'm on the other line. May I call you back? Thank you; good-bye.

   You: Thank you for waiting, Sara.

B. You: Excuse me, Sara. The other line is ringing. I'll be back to you only if I don't prefer to speak to the person on the other line.

   You: (go to call waiting call) Hi, Tess. I'd much rather speak to you than Sara. Let me get her off the other line. Hold on.

   You: Sara, I'll call you back another time. (Hangs up.)

Polly and Molly

Use your favorite color to color the telephone which is next to the telephone conversation that shows the best manners. Polly answers the phone each time.

Polly: Hello.
Caller: Hi. May I speak to Molly?
Polly: May I ask who is calling?
Caller: Yes. My name is Shari.
Polly: Hold on just a moment. I will go and get Molly.

What's mannerly? _____

What's not mannerly? _____

Polly: Hi.
Caller: Hi.
Polly: What do you want?
Caller: Let me speak to Molly.
Polly: (screams) MOLLY, TELEPHONE; HURRY UP, SLOWPOKE!

What's mannerly? _____

What's not mannerly? _____

Polly: Hello.
Caller: Hello. May I speak to Molly?
Polly: Who is this and what do you want her for? (giggles)
Caller: I want to know if she wants to come over today.
Polly: I think she is already busy.

What's mannerly? _____

What's not mannerly? _____

Polly: Hello.
Caller: Hello. May I speak to Molly? (mumbles)
Polly: Who?
Caller: Molly.
Polly: (chewing gum and drinking soda) Hold on.
Polly: (shouts) MOLLY, TELEPHONE!
Polly: (stays on line and listens)

What's mannerly? _____

What's not mannerly? _____

Discuss with your teacher, classmates and parents what makes each telephone conversation either mannerly or unmannerly. Remember it is not mannerly to chew gum, drink, eat food or scream while on the telephone.

GA1422

Chapter 8

How to Dress for Success

Keeping on Track

When you find a word in this chapter which you don't know, circle it in red and write it below. Then look up the word in the dictionary. Write the meaning next to the box.

Words	Meaning
1. _____	_____
2. _____	_____
3. _____	_____
4. _____	_____
5. _____	_____
6. _____	_____
7. _____	_____
8. _____	_____
9. _____	_____
10. _____	_____
11. _____	_____
12. _____	_____
13. _____	_____
14. _____	_____
15. _____	_____
16. _____	_____
17. _____	_____
18. _____	_____
19. _____	_____
20. _____	_____
21. _____	_____
22. _____	_____
23. _____	_____
24. _____	_____
25. _____	_____

When you have found all the meanings to the words, make a word search for your classmates. Use a separate sheet of paper. Put your name on the back of the paper.

Have your teacher collect the papers and pass them back out. Solve the word search you get. When everyone is finished, turn your paper over, find the classmate who designed it, and ask your classmate to see if you found all the secret words.

93

GA1422

Paula or Harvey?

Choose Paula or Harvey to take shopping. Draw Paula or Harvey's face and hair and then cut him/her out. You will be taking him/her shopping and buying the right clothes for the right events.

Dressing Up: Dressing Down

Help Harvey or Paula to dress the right way for his/her following event. Ask him/her a few important questions.

Where is he/she going and what will he/she be doing?

What is the weather like?

The answers to these questions will help him/her find the appropriate outfits.

Casual clothes are for everyday events like school, home, play, shopping, circus.

Dressy clothes are for more formal places like theater, parties, dances, weddings, etc.

Look in your closet and see if you can pick out your *casual* clothes and your *dressy* clothes. What makes them different? Which do you enjoy wearing more? Can you feel comfortable in either?

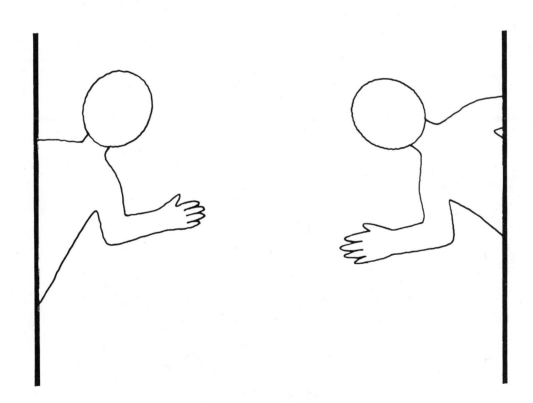

Shopping Spree

Both Harvey and Paula have to go to the following event. Cut out the appropriate clothes for him/her to buy. Remember the shoes as well as accessories. Put the clothes on the cutout figures that you cut from page 94.

Event—A school dance

GA1422

Good Habits

Make sure to remind Paul or Harvey to do the following before going out:

brush and floss teeth
shampoo and comb hair
take a shower or bath
groom finger and toenails

Add others.

_____

_____

_____

_____

Also remind them of the following good habits:

don't pop gum
no gossiping
good posture
no bad language
no yelling in inappropriate places
no showing off

Add others.

_____

_____

_____

_____

GA1422

Chapter 9

What Are Good Party Manners?

GA1422

Keeping on Track

When you find a word in this chapter which you don't know, circle it in red and write it below. Then look up the word in the dictionary. Write the meaning next to the box.

Words	Meaning
1. _____	_____
2. _____	_____
3. _____	_____
4. _____	_____
5. _____	_____
6. _____	_____
7. _____	_____
8. _____	_____
9. _____	_____
10. _____	_____
11. _____	_____
12. _____	_____
13. _____	_____
14. _____	_____
15. _____	_____
16. _____	_____
17. _____	_____
18. _____	_____
19. _____	_____
20. _____	_____
21. _____	_____
22. _____	_____
23. _____	_____
24. _____	_____
25. _____	_____

When you have found all the meanings to the words, make a word search for your classmates. Use a separate sheet of paper. Put your name on the back of the paper.

Have your teacher collect the papers and pass them back out. Solve the word search you get. When everyone is finished, turn your paper over, find the classmate who designed it, and ask your classmate to see if you found all the secret words.

GA1422

The Last Sleep Over

Luke is eating dinner and spending the night at his friend Charlie's house. Why do you think Charlie's mother will not let him sleep over again? Circle the reasons below and discuss with your teacher, classmates and parents.

Why doesn't Luke get invited to Charlie's again? Circle the possibilities.

He doesn't greet his hostess.
He is disrespectful of property.
He is demanding.
He grabs.
He doesn't ask permission.
He does not show appreciation.

GA1422

Sleep Over Etiquette

Teach Luke some manners. Show him what good manners look like when you are at someone else's home for dinner and sleep. Draw your own pictures of Sara staying at Helen's home. Make it different from Luke's sleep over.

Why does Sara get invited to stay at Helen's again?

_____

She _____   _____

_____   _____

_____   _____

_____   _____

_____   _____

_____   _____

_____   _____

_____   _____

_____   _____

GA1422

Being a Good Party Giver

Make believe you are giving a party. Fill in your invitation below.

Please come to my _____ party.

Date: _____

Place: _____

Time: _____

Given by: _____

Bring: _____

RSVP

What does the *RSVP* mean? _____

Why do you think it is better to mail invitations than to give them out at school?

_____

Why would you not want to discuss your party (or other parties) in front of someone not invited?

_____

GA1422

Guest Etiquette

Use your favorite colors to color the gifts that describe good guest etiquette at a party. Discuss.

I called at the last minute to say I couldn't come.

I was not too rough or wild.

I left early without saying good-bye.

Send or give a gift even if you do not attend (although invited).

I thanked the host/hostess and parents before leaving, shook their hands and made good eye contact.

I responded to the invitation.

I spoke to everyone at the party including the host/hostess.

I took part in all the activities.

I bought a gift that I knew the host/hostess would like.

I dressed appropriately.

I forgot to bring a gift.

I wandered through the hostess' home.

GA1422

Host/Hostess Etiquette

Color the balloons that describe good host/hostess etiquette your favorite colors. Discuss.

I walked each guest to the door and said good-bye.

I got the biggest piece of cake.

I fought with a guest.

I spoke to some guests and not to others.

I wrote thank-you notes to everyone.

I behaved well.

I made sure no one felt left out by talking to everyone and including them.

I opened only a few gifts, not everyone's.

I helped my parents set up and clean up for the party.

I hung up guests' coats and told them where they should go to join the others.

I said "Thank you" as they handed me presents and showed excitement as I opened the gift.

I greeted every guest at the door and introduced my friends to each other.

Party Etiquette

Samantha invited fifteen of her friends to her birthday party. This was the most exciting day of the year for her. Her party was planned for April 3rd. By March 28th only six of her friends called to say whether or not they would be attending.

Samantha decided to call those who did not call. A few said they weren't sure, some said they forgot the date and had thrown out the invitation, others said they would be there. One friend said she would come only if Samantha was giving prizes to everyone.

By the end of all the phone calls, Samantha was sure ten people were coming. Samantha and her mother prepared the food and baked a cake. Her excitement was high. Finally, April 3rd arrived. Only six people showed up. Two called and canceled at the last minute and the other two friends never called. The party was lots of fun and there was a lot of extra food since not everyone came.

Samantha opened her presents. She received only four gifts. Two people came without gifts. Samantha had a good day but felt disappointed.

What do you think Samantha felt disappointed about? Why? _____

_____

Make a list of all the unmannerly behaviors exhibited by her friends and how that caused Samantha to feel disappointment. _____

_____

Now make a list of manners that should be used when you are invited to a party.

_____

_____

_____

_____

_____

_____

On Your Mark...Get Set...Go

Have a contest with your classmates. See who can make the longest list of what would be mannerly behavior at each of the following events. You have two minutes for each. On your mark...get set...go.

At a Sleep Over Party For example, be quiet so others can sleep.	**Halloween Party** For example, don't be rough.
Museum For example, don't touch.	**In a Store** For example, no running or shouting.
On Elevators For example, give people room to get out.	**Planes, Trains** For example, sit in your seat.
Church or Synagogue For example, no giggling.	**Movies or Theaters** For example, no munching loudly on food.